Letter your Way to Positivity
A BRUSH LETTERING WORKBOOK

All rights reserved.
No part of this book may be reproduced in any form without written permission.
Copyright © 2020 by Lettering Creations.

Hello there!

From the moment you first picked up a marker and lettered that first stroke, you became a hand letterer. That's right; you might not be as experienced as others in the art of modern calligraphy, but you've undoubtedly been bit by the bug (or will be soon!). Don't worry, it's happened to all of us creative types. And it's a good thing. It's that first inkling that there's something to be created and you're just the one to do it! The best part? When it comes to art, everybody's is different. But it's still art. It's still a form of self-expression. And it still matters.

Whether you're a beginner to brush calligraphy, an expert, or somewhere in between, you'll likely agree it's always fun (and stretching!) to letter new words while practicing those same, familiar strokes. What better theme to practice than that of positivity?

Now, we're not talking that toxic kind of positivity where you feel pressure to paste on a smile, feel happy all the time, or share only the good parts of your life. Sure, optimism has its place, as does keeping a positive outlook when faced with adversity. However, in this workbook, we'll focus on the positivity that leans more toward holistic and less towards hashtag blessed in that superficial way.

That means, you'll be lettering words that will serve as truths. Truths of who you are and what you can accomplish. Reminders of self-care. Encouragements. And permissions to feel all your feelings. There is power in words and we think you'll find these words will stay with you throughout the day, long after your markers are put away.

This workbook is a way to practice your art. But we hope you'll also consider it a practice in mindfulness. Lettering itself is therapeutic and lettering life-giving words is its own kind of healing. You'll be lettering your way through the alphabet, but in a way that truly motivates you each day. We sincerely hope you enjoy the journey!

Recommended Pens: Tombow Fudenosuke Brush Pen, Crayola Super Tips, or Sharpie Brush Pen

Instructions: Hold your brush pen at a 45° angle. Apply light pressure on the upstroke and heavy pressure on the downstroke. Remember, practice makes progress. Consider using tracing paper to reuse this book. Try developing your own style. And most importantly, have fun expressing yourself creatively!

abundant

achieve

acknowledge

adore

On my mind and in my heart:

adventure

aligned

attentive

authentic

On my mind and in my heart:

bliss

bountiful

brave

calm

On my mind and in my heart:

capable   *capable*

captivating   *captivating*

centered   *centered*

confident   *confident*

On my mind and in my heart:

connected

considerate

courage

create

On my mind and in my heart:

desire   *desire*

determined   *determined*

discerning   *discerning*

dream   *dream*

On my mind and in my heart:

dynamic *dynamic*

embrace *embrace*

encourage *encourage*

engaging *engaging*

On my mind and in my heart:

enthralling   *enthralling*

exquisite   *exquisite*

flourish   *flourish*

focus   *focus*

On my mind and in my heart:

friendship *friendship*

fulfilled *fulfilled*

generosity *generosity*

glowing *glowing*

On my mind and in my heart:

grace   *grace*

gratitude   *gratitude*

harmonious   *harmonious*

healing   *healing*

On my mind and in my heart:

imaginative

inspired

introspective

intuitive

On my mind and in my heart:

kindness

limitless

lovely

magical

On my mind and in my heart:

manifest   *manifest*

meditate   *meditate*

mindful   *mindful*

motivate   *motivate*

On my mind and in my heart:

nurture   *nurture*

optimistic   *optimistic*

passionate   *passionate*

peaceful   *peaceful*

On my mind and in my heart:

persevere

powerful

qualified

relax

On my mind and in my heart:

satisfied   *satisfied*

serene   *serene*

sparkling   *sparkling*

spiritual   *spiritual*

On my mind and in my heart:

strong

tenacious

thankful

thrive

On my mind and in my heart:

tranquil   *tranquil*

trust   *trust*

unique   *unique*

valued   *valued*

On my mind and in my heart:

vibrant

whole

worthy

zeal

On my mind and in my heart:

Letter your own!

Letter your own!

Letter your own!

Letter your own!

www.ingramcontent.com/pod-product-compliance
Lightning Source LLC
Chambersburg PA
CBHW080910220526
45466CB00011BA/3541